Stephen Mackey

Miki

Hodder
Children's
Books

A DIVISION OF HACHETTE CHILDREN'S BOOKS

KT 0933872 1

A LONG TIME AGO AND VERY FAR AWAY, THERE WAS A PLACE
THAT WAS ALWAYS COLD AND DARK.
NOTHING GREW IN THIS ICY WORLD.

'I wish we could find just a little tree,'
said Miki to Penguin.

At once a little tree sprang up in front of them.

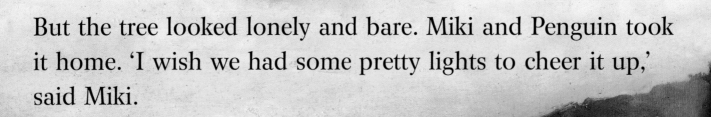

But the tree looked lonely and bare. Miki and Penguin took
it home. 'I wish we had some pretty lights to cheer it up,'
said Miki.

A string of fairy lights suddenly appeared. Miki draped them over
the little tree. 'If only we could make them twinkle,' she said.

The very next moment a twinkle machine appeared. Penguin
climbed aboard and pedalled faster and faster. The little lights
began to glitter, throwing sparkly beams over the snow.

But soon Penguin's feet were tired and sore. The pretty lights faded.
'We need someone stronger,' he sighed.

Miki and Penguin jumped. Polar Bear appeared from nowhere. He was
the strongest creature in the land and beside him was a windmill.
Polar Bear huffed and puffed and the little lights shone bright...

...but even the strongest creature can run out of breath.
Soon the three friends were in darkness again.

'I wish,' said Miki, as she fished for supper,
'I could catch a star. A star would
shine forever.'

All of a sudden there was a big tug on
her rod...

...and Miki was gone!

'Help!' called Penguin.

Polar Bear looked into the fishing hole.
Miki was nowhere to be seen.

But down in the deep blue ocean Miki
was safe in the magic of midwinter eve.
A gentle giant was taking her on
a journey.

She gazed with awe at the strange,
wonderful creatures. There were sea
urchins, eels and…

...JELLYFISH!

'Oh, dear!' cried Miki.
But he only wanted to show
them the way. He waved
his tingly-tangly tentacles.

'We're here,' said the gentle giant.
Miki dreamily floated down until
she reached the ocean floor.

Back on the ice, Polar Bear bravely decided to dive down
to search for Miki.

Down, down he went, but there
was no sign of his little friend.

On the ocean floor, Miki had fallen asleep, safely snuggled inside a sea flower. She was awoken by a gentle tickle.

A tiny octopus danced in front of her. 'Come with me,' he said.

Miki parted the petals. A wonderful sight met her eyes.
In front of her were a hundred twinkling stars!

Back on the ice Polar Bear popped back through the hole.
'No sign of her,' he sighed.
'I wish I could dive down,' said Penguin.

At once Penquin found himself dressed in a little penguin diving suit.
'Lower me down, Polar Bear,' he cried.

Down he went. All the time he looked about him calling out for his friend, but his voice was too small to be heard.

Penguin had never been so deep in the sea before.

The watery world was full of strange and fearsome creatures.
'Pull me up, Polar Bear!' he cried.

Polar Bear hauled him up just in time.

'No sign of her,' said Penguin sadly.
'But we must never give up.'

At the bottom of the ocean the magic was wearing thin.
Miki knew it was time to go home. The tiny octopus
took her to his mother.

Polar Bear was just getting ready to search again when…

...there was a rumble, a splinter and a crack!

The little fishing hole was opening up…

...bigger and bigger.
The ice started to move
beneath their feet and
the ground heaved and
shattered!

And the biggest creature the friends had ever seen shot out of the fishing hole!

There, nestled safely in its long arms, was Miki.

Just in time, for it was nearly midnight and the magic was running out.

And in Miki's pocket was a sparkling star.
A star that would shine forever.

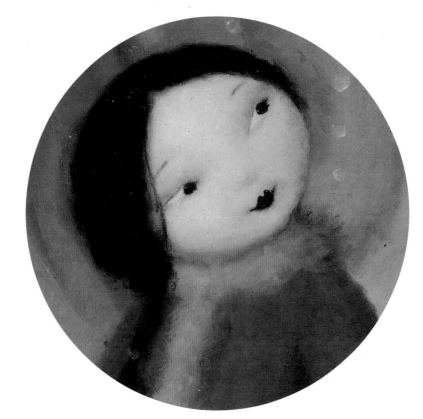

For Lily and Felix

Miki

First published in hardback in 2008
First published in paperback in 2009
by Hodder Children's Books

Illustrations copyright © Stephen Mackey 2008
www.stephenmackey.com
Represented by Lip International

Hodder Children's Books
338 Euston Road
London, NW1 3BH

Hodder Children's Books Australia
Level 17/207 Kent Street
Sydney, NSW 2000

The right of Stephen Mackey to be identified as the author and illustrator of this Work has been
asserted by him in accordance with the Copyright, Designs and Patents Act 1988.

All rights reserved.
A catalogue record of this book is available from the British Library.

ISBN: 978 0 340 95065 4

Printed in China.

Hodder Children's Books is a division of Hachette Children's Books.
An Hachette UK Company.

www.hachette.co.uk